THE GRAVEL LOT THAT WAS MONTANA

THE GRAVEL LOT THAT WAS MONTANA

D.A. LOCKHART

Mansfield Press

Printed in Canada

Library and Archives Canada Cataloguing in Publication

Lockhart, D. A., 1976-
[Poems. Selections]
The gravel lot that was Montana / D.A. Lockhart.

Some of the included poems were previously published.
ISBN 978-1-77126-200-2 (softcover)

1. Montana--Poetry. 2. Erie, Lake, Region--Poetry.
I. Title.

PS8623.O295A6 2018 C811'.6 C2018-905168-X

Cover Photo: David Mercer
Typesetting & Cover Design: Denis De Klerck

The publication of *The Gravel Lot That Was Montana* has been generously supported by the Canada Council for the Arts and the Ontario Arts Council.

ONTARIO ARTS COUNCIL
CONSEIL DES ARTS DE L'ONTARIO
an Ontario government agency
un organisme du gouvernement de l'Ontario

Canada Council for the Arts
Conseil des arts du Canada

Mansfield Press Inc.
25 Mansfield Avenue, Toronto, Ontario, Canada M6J 2A9
Publisher: Denis De Klerck
www.mansfieldpress.net

For James Pederson, the original mountain man.

CONTENTS

FROM THESE NARROW SHORES

Begin here, in this blue ribbon
of a river highway between nations.
A place birthed by Odawa fire dances,
cleansed in flames of the Nain Rouge,
reborn by the smog cast off by industry
of cars, fed by the steady motion of water
downgrade towards distant oceans. Here
nations grew outward, surrounding all
that came before. Here, the known world
begins in majesty, serenity, violence.
From these narrow shores we begin,
That which follows comprises all
we shall ever know, the feel of bare
feet on once-distant earth, defiant
grind of wheels upon interstate,
sing-song of wind in our ears.

A NATURAL VIOLENCE

The jack pine mangled
Tom Thomson and returned
to rest atop the granite
shield as waterline
was broken by a flesh puffed canvas.
This lake rings out
with aftershocks,
crests of cold flesh
hitting the empty shell
of wood. The canoe top-heavy
with oil paints, canvas, fishing line.
The pine seesaws.
Winds descending from James Bay,
jolt straggled limbs.
A half-rendered pine
rests atop a board
tinted with oils.
The pine groans.
The wind relents.
The oily smears
shadow the pine
and remain firm
despite the waves.
And the pine lunges
at high summer clouds
as the wind mounts again,
slamming a rigoured artist
into the side
of a red canoe.

THE SECRET LIVES OF JACK PINES

She told me her name was McKenzie
and we sat out like two limestone spires,
she thumbing shoelaces, and I counting waves
as they slapped into the dock beneath us.
Her name reminded me of the Prime Minister,
the one my parents knew as children.
Where that name should have felt sepia
and impossibly small, it shined red
like the verso of a 50-dollar bill. She talked
B.T.O, and all those legendary rockers
from the hundredth meridian and she was alone
huddled like a buffalo in a prairie snowstorm.
Across the lake, the pine trees creaked
with solidarity as they were moved
by a distant wind. Something crashed down,
breaking through the flatness between waves
some distance out. And I laughed because B.T.O.
was some other uncle's band and she, she moved
in closer while the waves slowed to a light tumble
and I strained to hear the distant secrets
of jack pines as they too bent into the wind.

BEHIND THE BRIDGE TAVERN

Behind that teal mess of a bar,
We greet an orange-blue sky
of a late summer night above
Waawiyaatanong, as we stand
alongside bins of used grease,
we burn an homage to rock
shows we should have seen, wait
for our Argentine cousin to make
his way back to our fiefdom,
from delivering a dead girl's yearbook
that he waited five years too long
to bring forth. Breaking between stone
casts of shuffleboard and choruses
of Ratt, Metallica, and Gandharvas,
we blow smoke skyward, shuffle a loose
grass dance, freed from that cavern
of the bar, for fresh air we filled
with Formosa vapour breathed between
words. Each line about the things we might
start up after this game, or the next.

We return to the bar when blue beats
an orange sky black. Well into the fifth
end, our Argentine comes back. He speaks
of Basillians wandering the campus nearby,
offers a strolling genuflection to a god alien
to this land outside here. Fresh air,
Rothmans, and the encroachment of night
had done much for our game.

Behind that teal blue mess of a bar,
in the middle of another Tuesday night,
where you would tell me, years later,
that you felt you finally hit the kind
of stride you wished your father had.

LOOKING FOR ARMSTRONG AT DOCTOR DISC, WINDSOR, ON

The snap, snap, snap of CD cases slamming together
punctuated the hunger your fingers hit the bins with.
A nervous hunger that jolted every move,
ended in quick smoothing of a single strand of hair.
Near Lou Reed you told me that you were pretty
damned sure you were going to marry that biologist
from Tennessee. And I agreed that southern rock
was something that we all had to experience
for at least a few years in our lives.
You hinted that for some people life choices
weren't so clear cut as musical genres and
anything but four minute packets of melody.

I went on to tell you about Americans,
how they were the childish heart of us all.
Without them, all we were was bubblegum
McCartney songs and a handful of waltzes.
From that Ouellette Avenue store we went
out into the first of our new year's snowfall,
you with a used copy of Bookends,
me with a water-tested Monk's Moods.

When that phone call came in from Rocky Mountain
House the better part of seven months later,
your voice scratched and distant like an Armstrong
and Hot Five album, I knew that the biologist
had been left standing in Knoxville
and you were hiding in that hiding place
where you wished none would ever go.

SUN RISES OUTSIDE THE AMBASSADOR BRIDGE TOLL PLAZA

Sun comes in, between
bridge deck and security wall.
Midway, St. Anne's turrets
pierce an arenaceous daybreak.
Here on ground that is neither
nation on these straits, there is
no drum, no fire to greet
the return of honest light
Only the tin-thin
scream of semi air brakes
giving out after descent.

Work here is motion
over control, traffic moves
as it will, cutting paths
through duty-free plaza,
through thin paneled gas pumps,
Absolut whisky sales,
and pretty-boy cologne ads.

Under the watchful gaze
the penned-in bait-n-tackle
shop scours this parking lot
for an absentee mogul
who erected barbed-wire
fencing and concrete highway
barriers on land forgotten
since a rebellion four decades
past. It sees cargo moving
between places, occasional toll
attendants tottering out of booths,
bringing cash boxes
to the middle manager
henchmen inside.

SIX HAIKU AT THE FORT WAYNE MILITARY MUSEUM, DETROIT, MI

(I)

beyond half-bent fences
Spanish War green paint flakes
waves from empty guard houses.

(II)

gulls bob in river waves
pushed off by a lake freighter.
dock posts slant toward shore

(III)

below cannon ports
river wind rustles young leaves.
tires ricochet through potholes.

(IV)

breeze through the trees
makes grass feel like bone.
vines rustle on barrack walls.

(V)

downed power line
uncoils on sandy desiccant lawn
northern water snake dozes.

(VI)

delta ’88 tires push down
mounded gravel with a crunch.
a radio plays Chaka Khan.

MIGIZI LOOKS BACK UPON WAZHASHK

This view become reversed, Migizi watching
Wazhashk, full, but curious, even February grey
makes the appetite for what lies opposite us, dull.
A river stretched between us; steam forced up
between fractures in a turtle shell of ice, rises
as if stoked by inner fire. Body mirrored by surface
ice rushes eastward to shallow wide-open waters
between nations. Know that geography changes people.
Borders make a mile a lifetime away, rivers are
that ethereal mass separating us, changing tragedy
to entertainment. We linger, our view empty
as late-morning is pounced upon by a howl of sirens
crying out in gun-to-temple love. Our footing is,
to be certain, exactly as wide as our maps make it.

CHASING THE NAIN ROUGE

We came to chase the Nain Rouge back into the river.
Each of us hammering upon pock-marked cymbals
and discarded paint buckets playing those out-of-tune
quadrilles that folded to the contours of long forgotten
Catholic prayers. We sounded as if this was our second
coming and our drive to baptize this little red devil
in shallows between Indian Village and Hog Island
was some way breaking a world in need of being broken.

We were told it had all been done before: Antoine
de la Moethe Cadillac in 1701, by Woodward
and his boys after the great fire of 1805, by line-workers
fleeing the smoke of 12th street in 1967. Every time
those upon the land changed that little devil found
a burned out hovel and slept beneath the ruins
he had left behind. We knew that history had a way
of repeating itself like a child learning their first melody –
it's all slaps and whistles and jibberish, yet sing-song.
But survivors rise up and true survivors don't flee
but reconstruct themselves in the way that hiding
beneath rubble or fleeing across township
lines could never manage to. We fear no red devil.

Robed in thrift store recreations of what each of us knew
that little French devil must truly look like, we marched
through the acres of gravel parking lots and the blocks
of what used to be the offices of our grand arsenal
of democracy. Each block pushed quadrille to dirge
to the certain groan of a post-bebop Marvin Gaye
infused cry. The kind of transformation that held roots
deep into decades of the wrong people writing
someone else's history. Amidst a third wave of trumpet
and clarinet and the folding of those asphalt-inspired

scales, we paused where Woodward met Joe Louis's fist,
knuckles swung northbound, halted by the long-line
motorcade of an automotive CEO as they returned
to a riverside penthouse from another overseas sales job.

NORTHWARD TO A BRIGHTMOOR BONFIRE

This night surges up Telegraph, away from Dearborn
wire-straight through half-lit neighbourhoods
of bungalows, coney islands, and cellphone shacks
to the outskirts of the city that each day we steal
as our namesake. Dropping High Life bottles at speed
from an inherited Saturn, we arrive bathed in shadows
that dominate beyond the last streetlights, fire turning
unfamiliar figures into hazed-out human echoes
of first-ring suburbs, unrelenting hold-out war camps
in a nation that thinks so little of them to bother
with even an occasional DPD cruiser or street sweeper.
Another night that we want to rage against what lies
in those shadows. Instead we find plain women
and escape through half-motions of love and charisma
in the only way hourly workers can pull off. We leave
before giizis burns open the Pottawatomi sky, we flee
visions of everything we couldn't be, visions appearing
solely in ozone-heavy blanching daylight. Wire-straight
we surge south into the comforts provided by another
shift pouring coffee, leaving behind Brightmoor's fires.

THE WARMTH OF FLESH

Winter descending now.
Wind pushing
black-tipped clouds over
Jefferson Avenue's distant shore.
I feel as though
it must be
1949
on Belle Isle.
I think of Philip Levine,
his nameless,
temporary Polish flirt.
Watching them swimming
out from here,
Hog island,
this island.
Watching them scissor-cut
in fresh industrial muck
of post-war Detroit.
Coming back cold.
Yet warmed by the
proximity of naked flesh.
The beach
like the river before me
abandoned.

I kick up chunks
of frostbitten sand.
Cold, alone,
the shadows
of Levine's long forgotten
encounter, haunt me.
Detroit,
more shattered glass now,
stares back.
Challenging in her battered glory,

asks to forget.
Memory
a sharp-edged reminder,
that these empty waters kill
in silence.
A suffocating absence
of violence.
In the gathering wind,
the black wing-tipped clouds,
pulling closer to earth,
I need to feel
a glancing blow of warm,
nearly divine, naked flesh.
Yet, I can't forget
the warmth of flesh
before it is consumed
by the bitterness
of the passing river.

A HISTORY OF OPTIMISM AT HART PLAZA, DETROIT

In the aura glow left by spotlights
caressing distant Ren Cen snake skin
she stands there, beautiful in the way
you've always imagined smoking
cigarettes at the lunch wagon would be -
just enough black latex and fish-net
to say that she's wearing something,
slouching on Hart Plaza concrete
you were certain Bill Bonds claimed
as his when he parked his Oldsmobile
in the Dodge Fountain after another
night of murder and special interest
pieces. She is alone in the resonance
of a Model 500 inspired DJ, shows
no inclination to movement. Rests
in a city where said word is a sin.

You are near certain she looks towards
you then drinks down Vitamin water.
Her gaze that moves past you saying,
she's seen everything from the New Dance
Show to impossible pleats left by Singleton's
Cleaners. Music rises, modulated waves
like tires on pock-marked freeways
and for one, maybe two whole minutes
you feel at home, in transit, moving
at 70 mph up the Lodge to the highlands
where money goes to retire, nestles
itself in the tall trees like wood ducks,
grey squirrels, and deer blinds.

With a whip of her Napoleonic blue
hair extensions, know she's moved on
in the way one must when you call
home a place where the motion between

townships is the song that most fills
your time, any stoppage and news
rings in like Mort Crimm explaining
another factory has shook its roots
free and moved to places once known
through family vacation photos.

Offbeat, between two breakdowns,
she reaches her elfish hand behind
her, fishes out her skin tight underwear,
finishes with a thick stream of neon
spit onto the ground beneath her.
She leans forward, falls into a post
third shift trot you feel certain
proclaims this is a city that can't fail.

REBELLION OUTBREAK OUTSIDE THE PLYMOUTH TOWNSHIP KROGER

We ignited fireworks
in that Kroger parking lot.
We watched as the fuse
burnt towards cardboard
inside the zinc-plated cage
of a shopping cart and pushed
them through nickel-metal hydride
shadows towards the cart corral.

We lit them believing freedoms
aren't freedoms unless practised
with combustion and detonation.
And practice is that sort of path
newcomers such as us must follow
to become free, like everyone
who had sought their gilded future
in the cycles that started or ended
in bungalows of factory-working
generations, cycles powered on
pitchers of Stroh's and low-grade
pool hall victories that made
workday Mondays feel like
an inevitability worth
building a city around.

As that cart exploded into
a slow-rolling bazaar, we
hoped for some raw recognition
of all that we had wanted
to throw in this world's face.

In the soot and powder afterglow
of our shopping cart rebellion
we watched as a man in a

Super Bowl XXIII t-shirt and ball cap
loaded his grocery bags into his Chrysler
and drove off north in the yellowing lights
of Sheldon Road, not bothering with
the smoldering remains of another
burnt-out rebellion.

DOWNRIVER TO THE OLD IRON WORKS

Through the yellowing light
draped over bent sidewalks,
angled street posts, and sun-
hardened grass medians, drawn
by demands of youth, a car,
and the soundtrack of one
record store clerk who refused
to believe in the death of vinyl,
we push down river amidst
shadows of long-shuttered iron
works. We become the passing
body of refined plastic caught
in currents between used car lots
and barbed wire topped fences
that separates living from dead
in this industrial riverside sprawl.

Northward ascending Jefferson
toward the vacant metal din
of Zug Island, flowering pillars
of industrial steam works we could
taste, the softening edges of our world
coloured by inhaled clouds of crisp
burnt tea; sulphur greets the baptized.

At the drawbridge gates we stop,
witness the city skyline that fueled
the American century through empty
lots where lunch wagons and night shift
union stewards once held sway. We see
in the horror and violence of nearby
mechanized refineries, their charred
metal spires carving ribbons of orange,
of blue, of so gentle yellow into
the oily black water night sky.

Realize that the susurrant passage
of time had deposited us here, against
that fissure that ran beneath
this bridge to the city beyond.
The threshold of which neither
of us could bring ourselves
to cross or turn away from.

THAT WHICH WAS NEVER MEANT FOR US

Below ground we became all those things
our ancestors promised. Played dress-up
with bolero hats, beer-league newsboys,
cheese-grater lawn chemical caps, mixed
each one with Bill Bonds six o'clock
news ties, chased it all with highball
Stroh's cans bought at the Van Born
K-mart. Know that we bellered at things
we could and wouldn't be. Line work,
union wages, and knowing every shift
completed would land you somewhere
other than in an old man's basement
wearing clothes not meant for you
on time that always belonged to richer
men who wore clothes made only for them.

FINDING LOVE IN GREASE CAKES AT CARTER BURGER, DEARBORN, MI

Let light sprinkle through
these grease caked windows,
tilt shine this aluminum
wrapped counter-service
burger shack built on pocket
change from shift workers
and fall awkward like a f-nine
into a Robert Fick right field
glove because not all of us
need be franchise players,
but must be remembered
for the manner we hold places
for those that must come to shine
in a town where bowling alleys
and drive-in theatres carry on
as if LBJ and his beagles never
gave way to Nixon and Kissinger.
Through mid-winter warmth
cast by this diffuse caress
from kishux, feel that love begins
with the fast flip of a beef patty
one-thirty-second of a pound,
flows in the juices that steam
up from the blacktop beneath
them. Each one slid expertly
upon sugar-sweet white bread
buns, the warmth unleashed
again in each gentle chew. Know
this is love, light in winter dark
for a city of shift work and fat
that congeals in places one
would never hope for, finds home
in the places never meant to be
more than union-rate piecework.

CONTINENTAL DRIFT: A STUDY IN MOVEMENTS

(a) we had heard of the drifting of continents and its associated premises at a coffee house in Plymouth. we had heard the theory from the guitar of an off-duty humanist. He sung it with the hint of an Appalachian whisky dialect, sweet but hot as an Alberta clipper moving across the lake.

(b) we had witnessed evidence of continental drift. staring off the third floor patio, smoking Pall Malls and weed above the orange glow of a rain mist dressed Pellham Street. we became mindful should the earth itself move. To the south and west webs of lightning unfolded above the trees.

(c) we had dreams of continental drift. we beheld them on summertime nights in identical neighborhoods transected by four, six, eight lane highways. we saw this steady movement in the passing of overhead lights and the reflections of highway markers between I-96 suburbs.

(d) we had discovered in the quiet times, alone, that continental drift moves in spasms. it comes in the grind-lock-slip migrations of plates. the potential for movement something that hangs like a threat of creation, the belief that all people belong in just one place proved false in nature.

(1) we had become continental drift. we awoke in the shadow-side ground-level room of a Quality Inn just inside Joliet. 1,390 high prairie miles, heat lightning, and rangeland cut up by electric fencing before us. we sang about antelopes, and stopped in Mitchell to take in a thunder storm.

(2) we crossed the Crazies at night, free of even distant street lights, Apsáalooke land itself layered around the reflected green and white of road signs; reminders that beyond the embankments there were no services; just ranch access we realized humanists fear mankind.

(3) we descended through the relics of earth and pure snow that punctured the tùkswi kishux dominated sky. drift became steady descent. we skimmed rock surface, as if nestling into the space we belong. you hummed an old soul tune you said your dad sang to you.

(4) we acceded ourselves to the valley; the land a flattened shield punctuated by the orange glow of sodium vapour light. beyond all was darkness. starlight and the bugle of elk lost to the way newcomers busy themselves bringing themselves to the land they've never known.

(5) we awoke the next morning to a cacophony of snow and thunder. bunk beds shared with Star Valley horse tamers, a night amongst cowgirls inside the walls of Gary Cooper's boyhood home, we reckoned the slowness of earth with quickness that life gathers speed, returns to the familiar.

(6) you met me beside the car on the street where we had first seen magpies. in that tëmetët shaped hat you talked up the film you had just seen. at night the magpies were gone, Olive street jaundiced in streetlight. could we know much about Gary Cooper or the marks we leave upon the land?

(7) I climbed out of the valley after the big sun of Montana had burned off the grayness of brushfire ash and the freshness of late summer snow. you talked about the beauty of days spent in the valley. like the river tides receding, I had to return you home before your next work shift.

(8) through Nebraska like a mid-sunrise blur of light and diesel exhaust. we ate green chili burritos at stagecoach gas station and noted redheads don't get up before noon. our West ended at the Missouri. We rushed through Omaha and that rolling tease of land that ended at Michigan City.

(9) me on the back of a mostly empty pick-up truck at three am in Dearborn streetlights. mostly buzzed and alone with the distant sounds of inbound trucks on the interstate. six hours till migration zero hour and most of the city burns on around me. humanists are prophets that lonely men follow.

INTERSTATE 94 THROUGH ROSEBUD COUNTY

These ascending plains
of Eastern Montana
are covered
in the dark film
of humming, hissing,
and crackling
of AM voices.
Distant lights,
anchored to
rolling carpets of prairie.
And they move,
glide, drift into
the humming glow
of dashboard lights,
become the voices
of rammed-through roads.

"Posedinik on second,"
gruff words tumble past
in paired lights. Through
them we know Jesus
owns a gun and follows
baseball on highways
that rocket past patchwork
lights, half-alive in darkness
extending beyond the touch
of this great Interstate.

Between the popping
of distant lightning strikes,
the radio growls
into a sanctity
of voice, amplified
by human twang.

Chants of White Sox
faithful give way
to waves of static.
"Jesus is the light
upon the road
to our salvation."
Lights hit markers
in spasm. Pock-marked
sign declares
"Beulah 33 miles."
More static, less hissing,
and the growl becomes the awe
of thousands
heard through the tin
of AM radio.

"They're sending
Posedinik home,"
declares a lightning-edged voice.
Beulah forms into bands
of yellowish lights
at the interstate's fringe
and is swung aside
as this highway through
high prairie and climbs
towards the Rockies.
The sounds of distant
sport overpowers
the solitary cry
of a Kansas-based
salvation.

JACKALOPES EMERGE FROM THE ROADSIDE IN MITCHELL, SD

Three hours outside Wall Drug
that has been approaching since
Council Bluffs, wind shakes gutter
grass like a grand entrance inter-tribal
proud in the way Lakota means Fuck
You Uncle Sam, I ain't running nowhere
our new day is burned into being
through kishux as she climbs over
eastern cornfields, surmounts off-ramp
strip malls, backlights this grass dance
into ethereal visions which allow you
to believe that when one decides
what was once home is no longer
enough, one must follow the arc
she leads across the sky, discover
what emerges from the edges
of maps we have to draw. Between
passing cars and the shuffle
of retired corn farmers across
this parking lot, one must be certain
that between the rustle of grass,
that antler-crowned jackrabbits
witness this ritual. Know too,
that stovepipes can't protect you
from rumoured gorings, statehood
is something transposed upon land
that reveals myth as fact only
to those bold enough to follow
the dances and motions left us
by a creator that sells you
neither five cent coffee nor all-
day breakfast and follows paths
laid out before even a single
memory. These grass reeds
shake with quiet aggression
of five-point jackrabbits.

CONSTELLATIONS RETREAT BEFORE THIS TRUCK STOP NIGHT

After sunset these prairies
hide their absence of rise
in the evenness of darkness.
Backlit Flying J road sign
declaring this strip of Wyoming
belongs to the constellation
drawn from diesel vapour
of long-haul truckers coast-
bound. Private showers, ample
parking, and 24-hour steak dinners
just rewards for crossing the space
between. In this September hour
you know you make your own
gospel and the only surety
of the upcoming season
is the gristle of your 2 am sirloin.
Here, under this portioned out
license plate of a settler highline
across Lakota land, that surety
carries the weight it must
before you sleep through till
dawn in a Ford Ranger cab
at great remove from the sign
that bleaches out the horizon
and expanse of stars beyond.

GRAVEL LOT ABOVE CROW AGENCY, MT

The breadth of land rolls out from this stripe of asphalt,
four lanes knifing through, walled in by up-thrusts of prairie.
Grasses sway as if fancy dancing alongside a heartbeat
water-drum, whipped about and tossed in concussions jettisoned
from distant mountaintops. The rhythm is subtle here
in the place neither wholly Montana, Wyoming, or Apsáalooke.
The blades dance, sway, chant, cry, slide around this circle.

This is not Moravian 47, run up to the banks of the Thames;
familiar, embracing, green with flat fields of ripe tobacco. This is
a postage stamp of the ways in which Indians must straddle worlds.

At Crow Agency, the land is golden, dry, immeasurable.
The Beartooths rise in rigid meandering terror. Cottongrass
clouds cap these mountains as they lie in wait. Cold exhalations
sweeping between, around, through grasses that line this gravel lot.

Apsáalooke, famous for their Sundance, hide from divinity now.
Sun straddled land around us, cloudless and dominated
by an ever-present vengeful and jealous god.
This Crow sun does not feed the lush banks of the Thames.

We must want those powerful equine Apsáalooke warriors
to emerge and gain prominence under the bleaching light
of Crow Agency. Some victories are forgotten even by the victors.
Shuttered away to eastern monuments, wind and sun and sky
filling their vacancy. Felt not remembered.

Yet, the shallow Little Bighorn River pushes through this land
of arid rolling hills. Meandering by scattershot trailers and dust
tossed by half-tons on their way to and from town. The river
is moved by the same rhythms that clatter the grasses together
and sway the loosened arms of our Ojibwe brothers, coaxing
the heartbeat from the water-drum. Spilling blood over its banks,

flooding hapless fields. And I rest here, in the slim shadow whisp
cast by the truck that brought to this place, above Crow Agency,
imaging the Thames and Bighorn meeting in distant sunlit pool.

KISHUX MAKES MOVES ABOVE THE HARDIN, MONTANA SUBWAY

Alabama comes through
from behind the counter,
sky turning a bruised purple
over the nearby ridge outside
the dust-blasted window.
Modern American Indian
Sovereignty lies beyond
as the great Apsaloka Nation
basks in kishux diminishing
at the end of roads settlers
drove through from
the Neutral Sea
to frost-bitten ends
of rain-shadow sage brush
high plains. Subway,
the second best way
to receive the sacrament
of eight pm Indian Steak
and white bread. Alabama
white-boy soul delivered
the way each on or off res
Indian pictures themselves
Running for a little snag
on their own lady. Behind
the veggie trays, the clerk
absently hums along watching
the nearby Carhartt, buzz-
cut worker like she knows
he's a cousin, But after a long day
of sacraments, that sort of thing
don't matter as much as it should.

THROUGH THE MAGIC CITY

And we cut across the top of Billings,
moving beneath its granite upper lip,
watch as lights simmer on and above
the Magic City. Three days on and

somewhere beyond the setting sun,
past Laurel and rising sharply
from the raised shield of earth,
mountains emerge from rolling prairie.

Inward bending teeth caked in shadows.

We move under the rim
onto the broad flatness of land
sculpted by the Yellowstone,
and we feel as one with the shadows.

Refineries refract internal light,
spreading starlight against purplish cliffs.
Our sojourn onto the bleached-out earth
of prairies closes behind us
in fading bands of color.

As we pierce the threshold
of the Magic City's petering body
we welcome the shadows.

Light drops away into bruised sky.
Grasses and sagebrush bleed
alchemically into mounds of decaying bison
and the peaks of Crow camps.

A Coltrane glide through Stellar Regions
floods through the radio

and all we feel in that track-marked song
is our floating has become stressed.

I'm pushing the car.

We want to be home,
away from the tops and valleys,
these highs and lows of a magic,
alchemical city.

Away from the openness
of this sage-ridden prairie.
Free from the burning lights
of the nearby refineries.

DON FRY DESCENDS INTO THE VALLEY OF THE FLOWERS

They say he arrived in a classic Plymouth
came clear down the mountain pass as if
Jim Bridger himself wandered in Ohio River
cool, breezed in with a leather jacket that made
Easy Rider look like Goodwill movie props
and an Audobahn wife that could cook
a valley into submission. It is said thunder
snow greeted their first morning, magpies
every damned one of them, came in
from as far away as Lewistown. They came
to learn the one part of creation that had
no likeness. When Don Fry found them
gathered in the parking lot of a workaday
shack of a bar that had been there to greet
the Apasloka, he declared with the crack
of an Olympia can like thunder through
the aspens that this was some fine land
and that none shall want for thirst and food,
at a fair price, in a valley that shall know
no equal to a gutsy commonwealth man
who greeted magpies and tourists alike.

THE SHAPES OF OUR LEAVES

We must know something of ourselves
from the shapes of drying leaves
on the dampness of fall sidewalks.

The colours of them, flush to grey-brown
and the pleasant crunch as they disintegrate
under foot. And we know that these trees

have followed us through our continental
drift because the Apsáalooke have no word
for oak tree and the ground shows off

the wonder of their leaf shape.
And as we make our way up Wilson
past the forever wishful Storey Mansion,

you remind me that aspens cling
in stands just outside of town
and that beetle blight has browned

the slopes around Helena. And I,
I try and count the years of the nearest oak
by seeing how close it has gotten to the sky.

YOUR SHADOW IS ALL THE HISTORY THERE IS

Here, beneath the open faucet
of Big Sky, where your sunset
shadow stretches larger by some
than the Bridgers beyond you,
more perfect in line than the Crazies.

Here, you begin and end
creation in the wide-open copper
of rain-shadow flats between
mountain ranges. Walk to tall
grass playing wheat past the last
curb at the valley Walmart. Shadow
outstretched atop waist-high stalks.

Look for bison tracks, Blackfeet
pottery, bullet casings, foil chip
wrappers. Understand that they
are there, every one of them. Know
too that the outline of what you are
reaches well up towards Saddle Peak
and vision always look to the sky
first and rarely upon that beneath us.

AS THE SKY FALLS ABOVE TRIPLE TREE

There can be no mistake
that the world placed us
in this caliginous parking lot
of Triple Tree to witness
the Perseids streak through
their final fiery descent into
the ridges of adjacent Bangtails

And the sound of AM radio
filled with conspiracists
made all the more real
as two hikers inch out
of tall grasses, warning us
of bears and mountain lions.
Lauren from Vermont,
slides her fingertips across
the green and white sticker
of a backlit dashboard that reads
"Don't Vermont up Montana."
We tell her that this place is
two-thirds looks and
one-third inheritance.
She knew neither applied to her,
and ignored those two hikers
with us and looked to a sky
thrown open in a moonless
night. All of us quiet
in dry anticipation
of burning space debris.

RYAN TALLGRASS ARRIVES AT THE FILLING STATION

With all certainty he arrives
from the fresh descent of winter
along the only road out of
town to Bridger Bowl after
the third beer is cracked.
Twin braided and eager
in the manner, he stutters
through informal Thursday
night greetings. Cover band
plays Danzig beneath a Pegasus
sign at this VFW post surrounded
by lumber yards and self-storage
and through bottle cap glasses
he feigns curiosity at music
you've come to see. Inquisitive
as we must have been seeing
cartographers on the horizon
and the sense that Creator
summoned us before their
presence, the distance between
covered by the well placed snap
of three Olympia and knowledge
that no Indian should drink
alone in a cow town after dark.

AT THE HEADWATERS

You walk onto this dirt shoulder
like you're in a Paul Newman movie
but with a John Wayne landscape,
This place you've always pictured
yourself in is the spit of land y'ed off
with angry water raging around you,
the gravel of dry land is the kingdom
that surely bears an oedipal curse.
You've come to the headwaters
where the Jefferson,
the Madison
the Gallatin
all become the Missouri
and fall down-grade
to the center of America.

And you know that Kerouac
had run through here
the better part of a century before
and in Benzedrine induced sharpness
proclaimed this spit of land
the center of all existence.

In high-summer dryness,
the type brought on by 14-hour days
and multiple weeks with no clouds,
this backbone of eternity
feels desiccated and spit-out,
as if any moment a brush-fire
might sweep down the banks
and sublimate all existence
into a single
spire
of a
dust
devil.

DORIS RATTLES HER SNAKE JEWELRY TO MOUNTAIN BLUEGRASS OUTSIDE OF NORRIS, MT

Long after Doris took
a shotgun to the rattlesnake
hillsides and twisted
their remains into earrings,
necklaces, brooches, this night
is poured open
as if from a valve
left open by a God
that respects free will
above the hard edges
of life. Our night is turned
open by a steady chorus
of a Jerry Douglas tune.

Between cold smoke snow
falling dry and furious
over the rain-shadow side
of the Tobacco Roots
and the lithium steam rising
from this wood bench bathtub,
you should know better than
to buy anything but gas
and road maps from highway
stands and mineral water
resorts. Yet you are certain
that this place is still every part
of a highway stand divvying
out mineral water and the healing
glow of kaleidoscope stage lights.

In falling 120 degree water
from the sprinklers to
the 120 degree pool below,
there comes the even-time thrum

of water drizzling against
itself and the sure motions
of two brunettes saddling up
to the sort of night that costs
more than a Bridger Bowl season
of wages, and the practiced
belief independence can't be
dissolved even in a steam bath
at the high side of this dry
gulch surrounded by bristle-
dry sage brush foothills.

THE DIVIDE RUNS WEST OF HERE

Scared away by the shotgun
clunk the bedlamite retreated
into the Elkhorns as if a bear
chased him from the town dump
day after labour day. Forty-five
minutes of besieging a truck bed
campervan brought him no larder,
at best an one-man spectacle
and the old man a story
about the lunatics that gather
near rain shadow hot springs.
You feel outside the bowling alley
this land empty is bad medicine
grey, quiet, worn as if a rodeo
king hung up their chaps years ago.
Even the Blackfeet skirt this place
and the worst creatures come out
of the forest when working men
pass through town looking for
a good soak and a spot of liquor
on the wrong side of the divide.

HIGH PLAINS WARRIORS CUT A NEW PATH ACROSS THE LAWN OF LANGFORD HALL

Freed from the loose grit
of tailgate lot dirt, back
country flapjack mix dry,
we rip sideways through
game day aftermath, cars,
coolers, the face paint marks
dignity of post-war revelry.
To be sure the things we do
must always be preceded
by the firm resentful voice
of a man in uniform reminding
us that nowhere in this town
can three Indians be doing
much more than passing through.

As that Red Lodge Apsáalooke
followed the path laid out
by a Lenape transplant, cheered
on by the Assiniboine warrior
that primer covered Dodge
half-tone tore a path through
land no treaty Indian could own
up to and for a solid two minutes
we all felt free like a Native
hadn't in Bozeman for the better
part of a century and a half.

Before the Pickle Barrel, beside
the United Methodist Church,
we halted finding that familiar
path laid down at College along
with the dumbfounded look
of the Loaf-N-Jug clerk as three
modern day Indians tore-off

towards the Bangtails, Willie
Nelson see-sawing through
fall afternoon about the time
stars fell on Alabama.

TASTE OF HIGH MOUNTAIN BEIGNETS

From inside this lukewarm Creole café,
we watch Subarus and Audis stream along
Main Street, ascending paths to ski tops.
We watch them through frost-covered windows,
exhaust trailing wisps of cotton, disappearing in crisp air.
Hardened cases moving against the bitter tongue
of this Montana winter morning. It's all cinematic.
We realize that these are the late ones, emerging last from
the glowing blue of the Baxter Hotel's snow beacon.
Inside the café, the air is less hungry, filled with sweet wafts
of chololo memories and places near oceans, snow unknown.
Snippets of bayou life hung safely from high alpine desert.
Our early crowd is here, not those that worship snow or cross,
but those that wish to eat, dreaming of vistas without snow
and ice, and all these expensive cars and designer apparel.
Framed Louisiana warms the interior of this wooden shack,
Creole rhythms with strong Acadian snaps, forgetting winter.
Sitting behind a palimpsest of bright paper ads and streaked fog,
we are welcomed by dissonance, chair upon floor and a voice –
"Joan, Richard, Emily," names cried from a lost waitress, circling
with baskets of white cray paper and flour-soiled apron. We
all wish to claim a divine pilgrimage away from stereotypes
of ourselves, our town. Notions of place sold to those born
without the taste of childhood forest fires and chokecherries.
Dreams of powder and bison are for tourists. They push upstream
as we await our names to be called forth, in our shelter.
Sun rising above Saddle Peak and it is not a warm sun.
A different sphere from the one that Maclean's divine soul
basked under. His gods, our gods, upon the back of cutthroat
trout, monsters lingering just below the water's surface.
Visible, but unattainable. It's all art now, gratuit, and still elusive.
January now, the headwaters frozen. Cutthroat still,
waiting beneath the ice forming clean past whitewashed resorts.
We all dream of trout when they're not in season, brushing solace,
at least those of us in this Creole restaurant, around this table,

at this time of the morning, hiding from the voracious air outside.
In front of dreamers like us, frozen in this misplaced moment,
that lost waitress finds us with three cray paper baskets. Smiling,
she drops them before us, supple mounds of powdered sugar
rest upon and melt from internal heat. Basking in ambrosial wafts
of steaming high mountain beignets.

BASEMENT GARDENER PREPARES FOR GRAVE DIGGER

For the lawn it was early yet
and the potatoes, he feared,
had the blight. From gardens
cultivated in basement rentals
he preached of how one brings
nature with them, talked soil,
the way worms from Europe
tore up earth once refreshed
solely in fire, discovered new
pathways in a landscape alien
to everything that creation
had left to them. The night
before us was to celebrate
mammoth combustion-fed
trucks paraded on dirt tracks
before beer-fed spectators.
Astonished by the speed
at which the quiet can kill
or spread what would be
natural, beneath a crushed
velvet JFK he wondered
aloud if Grave Digger would
make an appearance, gaze
fixed on early lettuce shoots.

BREW SESSION WITH ELK

We watched a family of elk
as they foraged the melting snow
of the golf course behind your rental.
All the while Aiden ran in prairie dog circles
declaring that he too will build homes
in this valley as he pounded his plastic hammer
into the edge of a sawed off stud
that you had brought home
before the snows' last fall.
And you stirred the mash
while it steamed
into the open air of the garage,
telling me that Cooper's Dry Yeast
does the same damn thing
as that designer White Labs stuff.
And all I could think of was how hard
it was to pull in a meal
from the low pruned greens,
even those put there by people
who could afford for their children
to play with golf-clubs and snowboards.

OFF SEASON IN GARDNER, MT

Standing beneath the gates of Yellowstone, the sky filled with rolled toothy clouds, we faced nature's refined grandeur. Behind the arch, the hills unfolded to bison and cliff-leaping rams, braying into the wind.

Or at least we imagined them brushing past us, pulled and pushed by the steady ice-tipped air. Around us, as the engine hums and clicks, empty cafes watch pondering the movements of approaching bison. Woolen humped figures lumber over hills, cresting twitching blades of golden pickaxe grass and are blasted by descending winds.

We stand upon pavement, cooked up by summer road crews. Bundled against angry arrivals, out of season, alone. Imagining, while the Roosevelt Arch sprawls overhead, stone upon stone, bracing a titanium sky.

"For the benefit and enjoyment of the people."

Read, but not uttered. Our eyes move from Arch to hills to empty storefronts behind us. The engine hums, drones and clicks. We watch. November at the foot of America's Park, the last best wild space available for a charge. Cheaper in off-season.

Snow coaches assembled in neat rows, orange and blue, rest nearby on gravel lots. Noses pointed at hills, awaiting winters eminent arrival. We too wait. And where there should be anticipation, only an empty rushing silence envelops us. Surpassing the mechanical hum, drone and click as high mountain winds course past, pushing against empty wooden buildings and carrying the chthonic scent of approaching bison herds.

RAIN FALLS UPON THE COPPER KINGS

Waiting in the parking lot
of the Copper City Safeway
and rain comes in bands
from heavy white clouds
draped like stigmata
from the outstretched arms
of Our Lady of the Rockies.

Butte's hollow cavern roots
pull water from blacktop,
through to the honeycombed earth
with a baritone gulp and all
I thought about was how misplaced
rain was in this wide open
sun-shadow of a town.

Know that life-giving rain
works more toxic chemicals free
from the mountains around us
and turns the fine dust of Broadway
into a muck that once subterranean,
collects in ominous silt pools
around the rusted-out cart corral.

Emptied out windows rise
in multi-story carved wood
and worn brick across street
jostled a little more
slanted into the degrees of grey
and white that pass from sky
to earth. Long quiet, you are sure
you can hear the faint trickle
of rain as it is taken in, slow,
unsteady like a tired-old heeler
being called inside for the night.

Thought of which, even amongst
the steady, steady fall of rain
made me lean hard against
the back fender of your Outback
because this sometime town was
and always will be haunted
by those things that
it would be known through:
copper,
rain,
and the want to fix
what someone else
had broken.

CLOSING TIME PROCLAMATIONS, BELGRADE LIQUOR

All the ways he could proclaim
this valley was the one hustle
everyone was fifteen years
late for, you were certain
that his was a testimony
every low shelf grain liquor
salesman longed for. Certain,
that better days lie behind,
comforted that one had known
what sunshine had felt like
before the price of living
went higher than the combo
of a lift ticket and fishing license.
Each proclamation a variation
on themes left us by eighties
action films, leather loafers,
and all the inevitabilities of being
a single dad hawking booze
and cleaning floors. Each night
locking the doors behind us
before heading off to the next
way to squeeze a dime from this
thin-soiled divot of earth, twitch-
heavy optimistic stride carrying
him to the white-walled Chrysler
and mostly satisfied snow-capped
mountain smile showing another
day has come to an end without
the sky falling, the earth running dry.

HIGH PRICE OF GETTING BY IN THE TREASURE STATE

Wine bottle balanced against
an outstretched web of fingers
his need to take measurements
of the weight of bottled liquid
and balance its density against
a midge hatch alongside the trickle
of the Madison River in fire season.
He pauses, falls silent. Midwestern
optimism tempered in his gaunt stoic
look is the reminder that he needs
to carry out a big city hustle on cow town
folk in a ski resort valley to simply get by.
Each move is made with a sommelier's
easy sell to a Bud Light millionaire. Loose
finger jingle and you know questions
of friendship, maybe pity, weighted
against the ounces of weed he sold
the store owner on the cheap to make it
even for those Napa Valley bottles
he traded up for river guides, car
repairs, and the carbon fiber rod.
Commitment is the price one
pays to the things one must do
in order to more than get by
in a place that values roots over
skills, craftiness over honesty,
and grunts over brash displays.

SNOWSTORM AFTERMATH

for John Powers

Again, we sat out
in the aftermath
of the snowstorm
and barked into the rosy clouds
that socked in our valley.

You danced like Jack White
under the Blackpool lights
and I sang like it was 1998
in the Lager House on Michigan Avenue.
But this was Church Street
and the cedar deck
that you had built in spite of
the cold, the snow,
and the unjust pain
of being working class
in a vacation town
for the country's wealthy.

We believed that poetry,
our words, could change
the world outside of here
if only those around us
could care about something
not written by long-dead Brits.

We were sure that this snowstorm
had blown down the Gallatin River
through the gorge from Big Sky
and like the sure steady weight
of precipitation arriving from afar
we too believe we could bury
every way that we couldn't fit
into this given corner of Montana.

Through the bite of cold,
that we smothered
in room-temperature whisky,
we talked up a world beyond
our powdered mountain town.
One built up from pastoral verses
of Heaney and the early mumbles
of Dylan's *Blonde on Blonde.*
Both of us unwilling to notice
that you can't go back
and all too fervent about
not remaining here.

AHTUHUK WATCH FROM HILLTOP OUTSIDE HELENA, MT

In the time before we celebrate
the arrival of north winds,
here, well after the first snowfall,
these western winds berate
brown hills, shake their stubble
of desiccate grass. Recall Mt Helena
beyond them, as she rises
to caress a diminishing blue sky
over a one-time boom-town
that won its boredom with fixed
elections and a willingness
to pretend it is exactly what it isn't.
A lonely patchwork of homes skirting
the city it knows so little of
lays dusted with ethereal powder,
haphazard dirt roads that cut
between ramshackle homes.
Brown compacted earth shines
through, overrunning, staining
the last grasslands between city
and national forest land.
Neither town nor ranch,
Neither consecrated nor discarded,
upon the furthest hilltop,
five ahtuhuk watch as you walk
this lopsided rectangle of streets.
Witnessing your progress, they gather
themselves and walk off towards
the north, over the ridge,
to the purplish sky
and highway beyond.

POOL BENEATH THE OLD BATHHOUSE

I wonder what I'm doing here,
soaking as old
Flathead slides around
the poolside in thick flannel.
He's been here all his life.
Not looking so healthy.

Our simmering water flows smoothly,
colliding with disappearing hillsides.
No sky, only clouds, steam
and sulfur.
Flathead says nothing.
"That's the smell of healthy,"
utters a bearded berry farmer
from down Oregon way.
He's the only other one
moving inside our shared tempest.

Yet, we know nothing
of each other but our forms
against dead thickets of grass
towering above snowdrifts
while wind fearfully shakes them
under a boarded-up hotel above us.

Plywood,
not so distant,
creaks in gusting flurries.
It's this twenty-foot cement tub
and old Flathead holding forth
in the enveloping whiteness of storm.

Mountains become walls,
sky ceases to be sky, we sit.
As visitors we've come

to a place haunted by memories,
of this place built on failed promises.
Old Flathead takes our five dollars,
drives up the vanishing road.

TRIBAL SCHOOL OUTSIDE OF HOT SPRINGS, MT

Pure even landscape stretches in all directions
as we move upon a single ribbon of black asphalt.
Ignorant as to how it cuts an insignificant grey line
across this freshly dusted virginal white plateau.

We slice downhill along that line and disappear
upon a dark cut ribbon of hard packed rock.
The earth a snow-folded hulk, thick with clouds.
Evenness that distorts every sense as we gage space
in numbness. Sporadic sagebrush emerges, snowy.

Harshly erected tribal school, worn wood and
english lettering waves from bobbing Flathead land.
It is unholy medicine pushing like dry sagebrush
from bends in the folded frost earth. We slice
past it, carried upon powder clouds pushed off
the darkness of road. We wonder about life
in the evenness of a squall on this plateau.
and move on to the certainty of Missoula,
and absence of Flathead upon the land.

CROSSING THE MEDICINE LINE

They gathered somewhere near here,
along a river that we couldn't see,
because they were moving north
away from the only piece of land
they wanted to know. Sitting Bull led
the Lakota across the Medicine Line
because death by unnatural causes
is something all people of this land
knew to be a death worth fearing.

Parched Hi-line wind gave hints
of mountains lined up to the sky
south of here. Realize canola fields
cover lodge pole pine footings
consumer buffalo hides and leave
us to Paul Kane paintings, silence.
Lakota knew they would not stay
along that shadow ribbon of river
because we are the places that we
must leave and fear is not enough
to make one deny the ways that
we know we must be. Always be.

Stopped, on TransCanada blacktop,
a couple hundred kilometers south
of Regina, we figured we too would
give that sort of northern drift a chance.
You were looking for pelicans
migrating inland from white cap seas.
And all I wanted to know was where
this line through grassland divided
us from the things we were.

GLOSSARY

Audobahn — neighbourhood in Louisville, KY.

Apsáalooke / Apsaloka — the Crow people. This is the term they identify with. Their current homelands are in the south central regions of Montana.

Ahtuhuk — Deer (pl) in Lenape

Giizis — Moon (Ojibwe)

Kishux — Moon (Lenape)

Migizi — Eagle in Ojibwe. The most sacred bird as it flies highest and closest to Creator.

Nain Rouge — The Red Dwarf. Specifically this is a myth from Detroit area. The dwarf is said to appear before major catastrophes in the area around the city. These include the Detroit Rebellions of the 1960s, the Great Detroit Fire, the Union Rights riots of the 1930s, and even before the city fell into bankruptcy in the 2000s.

Odawa — One of the Three Fires Confederacy First Nations (along with the Ojibway and Potawatomi). Had villages on the southern side of the Detroit River.

Tëmetët — Coyote (Lenape)

tùkswi kishux — Full Moon (Lenape)

Wazhashk — Muskrat (Ojibwe) Also slang for the mixed blood French that settled Windsor.

ACKNOWLEDGMENTS

The following poems appeared in the following journals. The author would like to thank them for their support of the work.

"Pool Beneath the Old Bathhouse"
Hawk and Whippoorwill, Winter 2010.
"A Natural Violence"
Hawk and Whippoorwill, Fall 2010.
"The Warmth of Flesh"
River Oak Review, Spring 2010 .
"Tribal School Outside of Hot Springs, MT"
Front Range Review, Spring 2010.
"Taste of High Mountain Beignets"
Naugatuck River Review, Summer 2009.
"Gravel Lot Above Crow Agency"
Front Range Review, Spring 2011.
"Through the Magic City"
Front Range Review, Spring 2011.
"Off-Season outside of Gardner, MT"
The Windsor Review, Fall 2012.
"Interstate 94 through Rosebud County"
pamplemousse, Fall/Winter 2016.
"Rain Falls upon the Copper Kings"
Cape Rock: Poetry, Issue 44.1/44.2, 2017.
"Constellations Retreat before this Truck Stop Night"
Welter Literary Journal, 2017.
"Migizi Looks back upon Wazhashk"
The Lindenwood Review, Issue 8,Spring 2018.
"That Which Was Never Meant for Us"
The Tulane Review, Fall 2017.
"The Divide Runs West of Here"
Camas, Fall 2017.
"The Secret Lives of Jack Pines"
Hart House Review, Winter Supplemental 2018.
"Kishux Makes moves above the Hardin, Montana Subway"
McNeese Review, 2018.

"Closing Time Proclamations, Belgrade Liquor"
McNeese Review, 2018.

"Finding Love in Grease Cakes at Carter Burger, Dearborn, MI"
McNeese Review, 2018.

"Rebellion Outbreak Outside the Plymouth Township Kroger"
Dalhousie Review, 2018.

D.A. Lockhart is the author of *This City at the Crossroads* (Black Moss Press 2017) and *Big Medicine Comes To Erie* (Black Moss Press 2016). He holds a MFA from Indiana University-Bloomington where he held a Neal Marshall fellowship in Creative Writing. He has received generous support for his work from the Ontario Arts Council and the Canada Council for the Arts. He is a pukuwankoamimens of the Lenape nation and a member of the Moravian of the Thames First Nation. He currently resides in Waawiiyaatanong on the south shore of the Detroit River.